40
Graphic Organizers
That Build Comprehension During Independent Reading

by Anina Robb

SCHOLASTIC
PROFESSIONAL BOOKS

New York • Toronto • London • Auckland • Sydney • Mexico City
New Delhi • Hong Kong • Buenos Aires

DEDICATION:

For my dear husband, Rob,
who encourages me to pursue my dreams.

Cover design by Josue Castilleja
Interior design by Holly Grundon
Illustrations by James Hale

ISBN: 0-439-38782-5
Copyright © 2003 by Anina Robb
All rights reserved. Published by Scholastic Inc.
Printed in the U.S.A.

8 9 10   40   09 08 07 06 05

Contents

Introduction

"This book is not for me." Tanisha pranced up beside me, waving her new copy of *Stone Fox* in front of her face.

"Why not?" I asked.

"This book is for boys. Anyway, it never snows like this [she pointed to the book cover] in the Bronx." Tanisha had a point, I thought to myself. How could I entice her to dig into this great story? Tanisha was from Puerto Rico and was currently living in a shelter with her mother and brother. Her father died in a work-related accident last summer, and Tanisha was still mourning this loss. A book about a dogsled race had nothing to do with her life. But I had suggested the story because I thought Tanisha could connect to its theme of overcoming obstacles as well as the feeling of hope in Willie's story. I knew that Tanisha had suffered like Willie. But I also knew she has a lively spirit that would not be kept down.

"Try it Tanisha," I nudged. "It's about this boy whose grandfather is very ill."

She interrupted, "My father died last summer." Tanisha looked at the book again.

"Why can't it be about a girl?" she asked. But not waiting for my answer, she walked back to her desk, reading the back cover again.

Tanisha was reluctant to read *Stone Fox* because she didn't think she'd be able to relate to the story: "This book is for boys." But since I knew Tanisha and her history, I suspected that she would be able to connect to the main character, to his strength and grief. And she did. Tanisha read and reread *Stone Fox* many times that year, each time finding something new that deepened her understanding of the book.

Teachers, educators, and parents continually ask students to read all sorts of materials: instructions, novels, newspapers, tests, web sites, poems, reference books, and a multitude of other genres. Hooking students like Tanisha to books during independent reading helps them build their skills so they can approach other reading tasks with confidence. The recipe for success is simple: The more students read, the more fluent readers they become. Regular reading builds vocabulary as students meet words in different contexts. Equally important, regular reading builds students' background knowledge, including their knowledge of people, places, nature, and how things work. The graphic organizers in this book will help you and your students get the most out of independent reading time, making it invaluable time for everyone.

The Benefits of Independent Reading

Establishing an independent reading program has helped both my students and me. Independent reading allows me to teach a heterogeneous class of students reading at many different levels. While students are eagerly engaged in reading—practicing their skills, applying strategies, building background knowledge—I am free to meet and conference with individual students. Children who wrote "I hate reading" on their reading surveys now protest when the lights flash signaling the end of independent reading. In an independent reading program, each student—from below-grade-level readers to proficient ones—has a chance to succeed, monitor his or her improvement, and challenge himself or herself.

What Research Says About Independent Reading

In addition to my own classroom experience, the research clearly demonstrates that independent reading helps all readers build their skills. Here are some highlights from recent research:

◎ According to Fielding and Pearson, recent research shows that less able, dependent readers and grade-level, proficient readers all benefit from independent reading.

◎ Richard Allington showed that when teachers give dependent readers chunks of time to read during the school day, they make more progress by reading fine literature than from completing skills worksheets day after day.

◎ The best way to improve reading is to read, read, read!

Making Independent Reading Work in Your Classroom

I have found it helpful to develop a classroom that is based on the independent reading life. Here are some things that I do in my classroom to facilitate independent reading:

- Offer students choices in the books they read. Let them select from several books at their independent or comfort reading levels.

- Help students find books that interest them. At the beginning of the school year, students complete "Reading Interest" surveys so I can get to know them better as individual readers.

- Present short but lively book talks and invite other teachers in to introduce new books to the students. These talks whet students' appetites for new books.

- Read Aloud several times a day. This shows your students how important reading is to you. Read Aloud will quickly become a treasured time in your class that neither you nor your students will want to skip.

- Share some personal stories about your reading life with the students. Tell them about a great book or a magazine or newspaper article that you've read.

- Reserve class time, 20–30 minutes a day, for independent reading.

- Encourage students to find a comfortable space when they read. Under a desk, on a pillow, and sitting against a wall are some favorite reading places in my classroom.

- Set aside time for students to talk about a favorite book with classmates. This discussion will inspire other children to read.

Every class has its own personalities, abilities, and pace. I hope that you will find, as I have, that independent reading is a great way to turn each student into an active, motivated participant in his or her own learning.

Getting Students Ready to Read

Helping students get ready to read can make a huge difference in their attitude toward a particular book. I encourage my students to set a purpose for reading every time, so they have a goal from the beginning. I share with them my reasons for reading and ask them to discuss theirs. Talking about reading builds excitement for the process and makes our classroom a vital place.

In addition to setting a purpose, I ask students to preview texts and use the strategies in Part II to get them ready to read. Taking the time to get ready to read increases motivation and is an important part of our independent reading program.

Idea Box

Why Do You Read?

To build students' motivation to read, invite them to explore their purposes for reading. Help them understand the many reasons for reading by asking them, "Why do you read?" and "How does it make you feel?" Follow up by sharing some of your reasons for reading, which may include the following:

FUN—Reading is a great way to entertain yourself.

EASE—Reading happens automatically every day. You read signs, headlines, and food labels.

MEANING—Reading teaches you new facts and helps you discover new ideas.

INFORMATION—Reading helps you understand the world around you. You can learn about current events and computers. You can learn how to play the piano or make a cake.

APPRECIATION—Reading a well-crafted poem, story, novel, letter, or article can develop an appreciation of the writer's craft and teach you to read like a writer.

Refer to this discussion often and encourage students to consider their own purposes for reading specific pieces.

Choosing the Right Book

When I walk into the local library and see all of the novels lining the shelves that run up and down the entire first floor, I get a little overwhelmed. How do I know which book to choose?

The first thing I consider is my purpose for reading. Is it enjoyment? Well, then a mystery novel or a romance might do. Or, do I want to reread a book that I didn't really get into the first time?

After I've decided upon my purpose for reading, I can narrow my selection. The key to success for all readers is to select books that they are comfortable reading. This way readers develop fluency, expand their vocabulary, and most of all, enjoy reading.

The Just-Right Book

Once students have found a book that interests them, the five-finger method is an easy tool they can use to decide if a book is "just right" for them in terms of reading level. Ask your students to turn to any page in the book they have chosen. If there are more than five words on the page that the student cannot pronounce or doesn't understand, the book is too hard. Suggest that the student save the book for another time. Or, if it's appropriate, you might offer to read it aloud to the class. Partner up students as they select books; having a partner ensures the students will monitor each other.

Demonstrate the five-finger method to your class by thinking aloud and explaining that some books are even too hard for you to read! Stress that independent reading should be fun and not a chore.

Think Aloud

Finding the Right Book

"Yesterday I was in the library looking for a book to give me some more information on taking care of my new kitten. I found a section of books meant just for veterinarians. I opened to the first page, but there were so many medical words and terms that I couldn't understand it at all. I became aggravated. Then I realized that the book was too difficult for me to be helpful. So, I put that book back on the shelf and chose another one that was for new cat owners. Everything in that book was clearly explained. Plus, there were great pictures that illustrated the directions. I knew that this was the book for me."

Honor Those First Responses

The first response readers have to a text is important and must be valued. The initial reaction is what bonds readers to books, often by linking readers' personal experiences to the characters or situations. We must validate these first responses, but then we must encourage students to take another look at the text and make observations and connections that can be supported by evidence/details from the text.

Model It

Moving Beyond the First Response

If students use evidence only from their own experiences in discussions of texts, prompt them to give detailed, specific examples from the story. Help them do this with these steps.

1. Ensure students can recall the plot. They should be able to retell the main events and identify key details. You can model retelling after Read Alouds, and encourage students to practice this skill during their independent reading.

2. Think aloud about how you find details in text to support a point you want to make. For example: *Cinderella's stepsisters are cruel. Here on page 4 one of them throws ashes onto the floor Cinderella has spent all morning scrubbing, and on page 6 they brag about being able to go to the ball and tease her about not having anything but rags to wear. Because of their actions and what they say, I believe the stepsisters are cruel.*

3. Model the difference between a general statement and a specific one from the text. A general statement tells; it lacks details. A specific statement shows exact details.

   Example:
   General: The room is messy.
   Specific: On the room's floor were chocolate cookie crumbs, dirty gym socks, last night's homework papers, and ants.

4. Encourage students to make specific statements in support of their ideas.

How to Use This Book

Once you've set the stage for a vibrant independent reading program, you're ready to use the graphic organizers. I organized this book into five sections. Part 1 and Part 2 can be used with any genre. Part 3 emphasizes applying reading strategies to different genres to deepen students' understanding and comprehension and to enlarge both their vocabulary and background knowledge. The goal of Part 4 is to build students' knowledge of the various elements of a wide range of genres. Understanding the structure and conventions of a genre improves students' comprehension. In addition, by understanding different genre structures, students gain the knowledge needed to experiment with a genre in their own writing. You can also use these responses as springboards for mini-lessons in writing workshop. Part 5 focuses on word study, an important component of any reading program.

It is not necessary to have students complete all of these reading response forms nor to step through them in consecutive order. View this book as a comprehensive menu from which you can pick and choose the items that will nourish and meet your students' unique needs.

PART 1

Record-Keeping Forms

The three forms on pages 13–16 help build students' motivation for reading and provide you with easy-to-use management tools that track student progress and interests. Students learn to pace themselves and take responsibility for their own learning, setting their own course for their independent reading life.

My Reading Agreement: A Contract

Use the first of each month as a goal-setting day. Have students commit, in writing, to the number of books they will read each month. The contract is a helpful tool for individualizing reading instruction. You can encourage struggling readers to complete one book or several books that are easier to read. You can challenge more able readers to increase the number or variety of books from what they read the previous month.

My Reading Log: A Record

Keeping track of books read is a great way for students to take responsibility for learning and for you to monitor the range and number of books read. As students log in titles, they have a concrete record of their progress. I find it helpful to set aside class time once or twice a week for students to log in books, and I encourage students to enter new titles soon after each one has been read. Ask students to choose **one** question to respond to for each book they read. Use the log and students' responses to discuss their reading during conferences with you or a peer.

Word Wallets: Building Vocabulary

Encourage young readers to build their reading vocabulary by collecting new and interesting words. Word wallets make this activity fun and keep the words organized. See Part 5, Reading and Word Study, for ideas and graphic organizers to teach students how to approach new or unfamiliar words.

Name: _____ Date: _____

My Reading Agreement: A Contract

DIRECTIONS: How many books do you want to read this month? Fill in and sign the contract.

My goal is to read _____ books during the month of

_____ .

If I can't meet my agreement, I will speak to my teacher at least three days before the end of the month to make a change.

Student's name _____

Teacher's name _____

Top Teacher Picks: Two titles you might enjoy (recommended, not required).

_____

_____

_____

Name: _____ Date: _____

My Reading Log: A Record

DIRECTIONS: After you finish your book answer ONE of these questions in your log.

1. What connections did you make?

2. What did you learn that was NEW or SURPRISING from the book?

3. What do you think the BIG IDEA or LESSON of the book is?

4. Compare yourself to the main character. How are you the same? Different?

5. What questions do you still have about the story?

(1) Title: _____

Author: _____

Date finished: _____ Question #: _____

My response: _____

_____

_____

(2) Title: _____

Author: _____

Date finished: _____ Question #: _____

My response: _____

_____

_____

My Reading Log: A Record, continued

3 Title: _____

Author: _____

Date finished: _____ Question #: _____

My response: _____

_____

_____

4 Title: _____

Author: _____

Date finished: _____ Question #: _____

My response: _____

_____

_____

5 Title: _____

Author: _____

Date finished: _____ Question #: _____

My response: _____

_____

_____

Name: _____   Date: _____

Word Wallets

DIRECTIONS: While you read your book, collect new or interesting words. Write the words in the wallets.

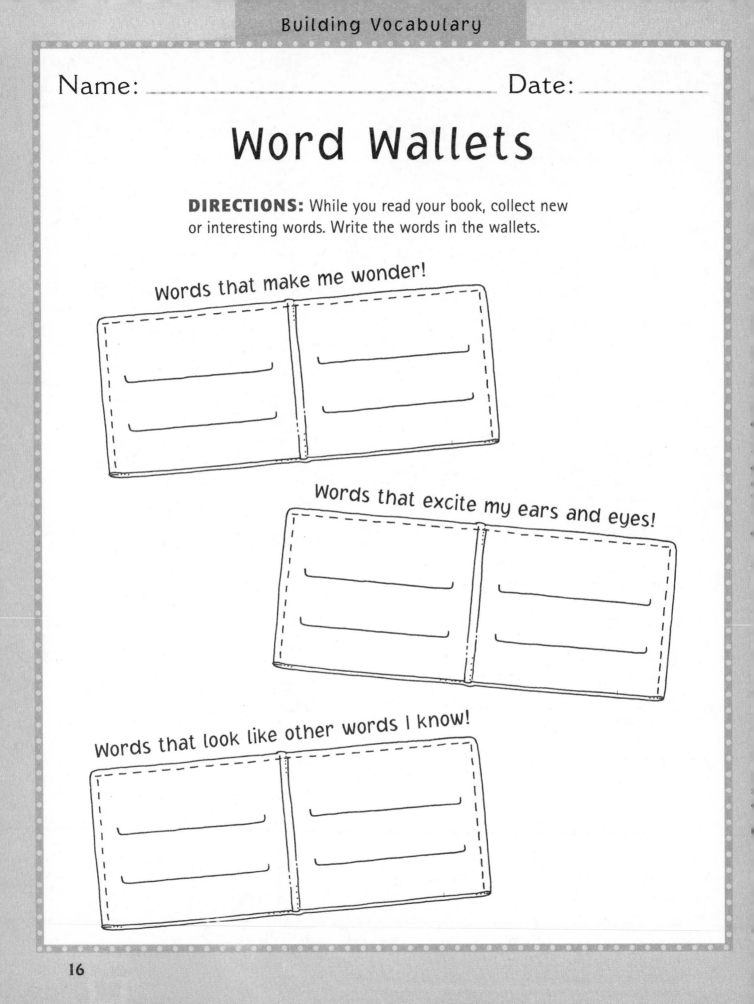

Words that make me wonder!

Words that excite my ears and eyes!

Words that look like other words I know!

PART 2

Getting Ready to Read

The graphic organizers in this section provide an easy, manageable way to get students ready to read. They encourage students to think before diving into a book. Calling upon prior knowledge and making connections to the text warm students up to topics and improve their comprehension. These organizers work with any genre and will help students get into the habit of previewing texts and making predictions about them and connections to them.

Get a Sneak Peek: Previewing

Introduce students to the strategy of previewing by engaging them in a discussion of how they choose a book at the library. Many answers will come up, such as: *I look at the cover picture; I read the back or inside cover; I look at the pictures inside the book.* Tell your students that what they are doing is called previewing. Previewing is an important reading strategy because it gives readers a sense of what to expect from a book or passage, and it helps them call up what they already know about the topic. Model and practice the strategy of previewing different genres with your students.

Preview and Predict Balloons: Making Predictions

Use this organizer before reading informational or narrative texts to help students collect ideas, words, and visual clues from illustrations or charts. They can then use this information to make predictions about the text. Now when they encounter new ideas, they will be prepared. They will be motivated to compare their predictions to what's in the text instead of being turned off by unexpected information or turns of events.

Hooked to the Book: Making Connections

Personal connections make a text relevant to students and help them see a reason for reading. Connections build a bridge between reader and text and help students move beyond their own experiences and relate to other people's lives and issues that affect the larger community and the world, such as poverty and the environment. Encourage students to use this strategy before every reading. This organizer will provide the scaffolding they need to practice making connections until it becomes a part of their reading strategies repertoire.

Name: _____   Date: _____

Get a Sneak Peek

DIRECTIONS:

1. Write the title and author of your book below.

2. Preview your book. If it has a feature listed in the checklist, put a mark in the box beside it. **Hint:** Not every piece of writing will have each feature.

3. Write what you think the genre is at the bottom of the list.

Idea Box

A genre is a type of writing. Some genres are

nonfiction: textbooks, magazine and newspaper articles, biographies, autobiographies

fiction: plays, novels, short stories, picture books

fantasy: fairy tales, tall tales

poetry

TITLE: _____

AUTHOR: _____

My Preview Checklist
My book has these features:

- ☐ headline or title
- ☐ table of contents
- ☐ chapter titles
- ☐ bold headings
- ☐ first and last paragraph
- ☐ boxed items
- ☐ bold words

- ☐ maps and graphs
- ☐ pictures with captions
- ☐ illustrations
- ☐ dialogue
- ☐ repeated words
- ☐ shape of a poem
- ☐ rhymes

Genre: _____

Name: _____   Date: _____

Preview and Predict Balloons

DIRECTIONS:

1. Read the title, back cover, and first page of your book; look at the pictures.

2. Write the title below.

3. Fill in the balloons with clues to what the book will be about.

4. Think about the clues you found. Predict what the book will be about. Write the prediction below.

TITLE: _____

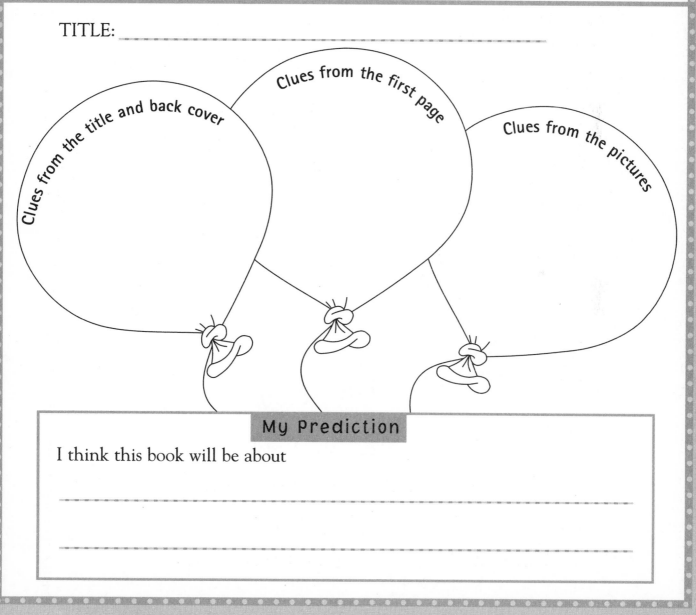

Clues from the title and back cover

Clues from the first page

Clues from the pictures

My Prediction

I think this book will be about

_____

_____

Name: _____ Date: _____

Hooked to the Book

DIRECTIONS:

1. Look at the cover.

2. Read the title, back cover, and first page of your book.

3. What do you think the book will be about? How do you connect to it? Write your ideas below.

The book reminds me of
_____
_____
_____
_____

The cover makes me think of
_____
_____
_____
_____

I have a connection
_____
_____
_____
_____

PART 3

Becoming a Strategic Reader

Strategies for Reading Fiction

Good readers use strategies to construct meaning and monitor what they understand and what confuses them. The five strategies in this section will help you teach your students to engage fully with the text while they read by predicting, retelling, questioning, visualizing, and using a storyboard. As active readers, students are better able to identify when they are having trouble and are aware of the parts of the text they need to revisit.

Read the Future: Predict/Support/Adjust

When readers make a prediction, they use what they know about the text and their prior knowledge to figure out what will happen next in the story or what a character might do. Explain to students that making predictions is what good readers do because it helps them to think hard about the story and to get to know the characters. Tell them that when they make predictions, they are detectives, using many clues to help form a hunch. Students can use the title, the illustrations, and the text as evidence to support their predictions. High-level thinking occurs when students find support for their predictions because they have to choose explicit and inferred details. After reading, ask students to confirm their predictions and adjust them if what they thought did not match the text.

Picture This!: Visualizing

Engage students by telling them that good readers make movies in their heads: The mind is a screen and the text makes images of things, such as what characters and settings look like. Research shows that readers visualize what they truly understand (Nagy, 1988; Vacca and Vacca, 1999). So when a student can visualize the text, you know that he or she has a deep understanding of its content. If students can't visualize a scene or event, it's a signal to go back to the text and reread.

Follow the Guide: Retelling

Encourage your students to retell when they come to the end of a chapter or to retell their favorite part of a story. Building this reading skill helps students improve their understanding of the text by helping them to focus on the important elements of the text. In addition, having students retell is a good way for you to assess their comprehension and recall. In your students' retellings, look for sequencing of events, naming of characters, description of setting and important details, and identification of problems. Remind students that if they have difficulty retelling, they should go back to the text, reread it, and then try to retell again.

Pop the Question!: Questioning

Questioning can be used before, during, and after reading. Before reading, questioning gets students ready to read by having them anticipate what might happen. This strategy builds students' motivation to read and engages them in the story from the start. When students raise questions during reading, they monitor what they understand, note what confuses them, and wonder about plot, conflicts, and characters. After reading, students can pose their own questions for discussion to help them explore the text in more depth.

Explain to students the difference between factual and open-ended questions: Factual questions have one answer while open-ended questions have two or more answers. Encourage them to develop more open-ended questions to explore texts after reading.

Sum It Up With Storyboards: Summarizing

Being able to summarize is an important skill for all readers. Ask students to be selective and choose only the main events when they create their storyboard. Remind them to include an important detail from the beginning, middle, and end. Summarizing not only enhances reading but also can be used by students to plan their own writing. Moreover, it is a great introduction to summary writing, as students focus on the essential details.

Name: _____ Date: _____

Read the Future

DIRECTIONS: Read the title, back cover, and first page of your book. Look at the cover illustration. Think about what you already know about the topic, the author, or the book.

1. Draw what you predict might happen in the crystal ball. Then write about it in the space below.

2. Sketch the clues you used in the space outside the crystal ball.

3. After reading, adjust your prediction so it matches the text.

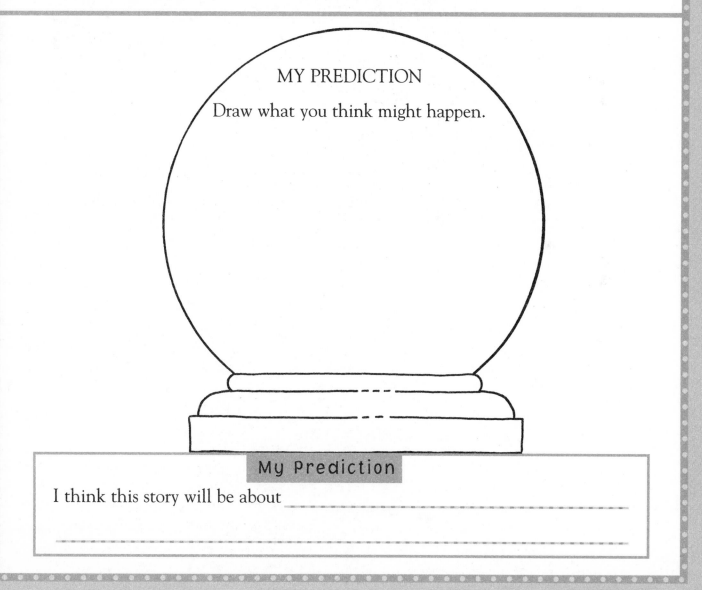

MY PREDICTION

Draw what you think might happen.

My Prediction

I think this story will be about _____

_____

Name: _____ Date: _____

Picture This!

DIRECTIONS:

1. Read the story or book.

2. Close your eyes. Picture in your mind two settings in the book.

3. Name the settings and draw them in the photographs.

4. On another sheet of paper, write about what you drew and why it was an important setting.

A trip to: _____

A trip to: _____

24

Name: _____ Date: _____

Follow the Guide

DIRECTIONS:

1. Read one chapter or two to three pages in your book.

2. Think about the characters, the setting, and the problem.

3. Draw and write what you remember in the boxes below. Use this sheet to help you tell about the story to a friend.

Chapter title or page number(s): _____

Who? _____

Where? _____

This character was important because

_____

_____

_____

This setting was important because

_____

_____

_____

Draw the problem in the box. Write about it in the space below the box.

The problem was _____

_____

_____

_____

The outcome was _____

_____

_____

_____

Name: _____ Date: _____

Pop the Question!

DIRECTIONS:

1. Before you read, answer the questions in the first box.

2. As you read ask yourself, "Is this making sense?" Mark any confusing parts with a sticky note.

3. Reread any confusing parts. Then, retell or put the confusing parts in your own words.

4. After reading, write down any questions you have and think about them.

Before You Read

1. What do I know about the topic? _____

_____

_____

_____

2. What questions do I have? _____

_____

_____

_____

After Reading

What questions do I still have? _____

_____

_____

_____

Name: _____ Date: _____

Sum It Up With Storyboards

DIRECTIONS:

1. Read the story.

2. Draw what happens first. Make a note telling about your drawing.

3. Add sketches and notes until you have included four of the most important or main events describing what happens at the beginning, middle, and end.

1. Note: _____

2. Note: _____

3. Note: _____

4. Note: _____

Strategies for Reading Nonfiction

By the time students reach the second grade, they have a strong sense of the structure of stories. This is a good time to emphasize reading nonfiction. Reading nonfiction expands students' background knowledge. It also deepens their understanding of the physical and natural environment and prepares them for reading the content area textbooks they'll encounter in the upper grades. In addition, more and more standardized tests focus on nonfiction selections. The graphic organizers in the following section will help you guide students to understand how nonfiction texts work and how to approach them in order to construct new understandings.

My Personal Thinking and Learning Record: Activating Prior Knowledge

A KWL (What I Know, What I Want to Know, What I Learned) chart is a great tool to use with your students before they read new nonfiction. This organizer invites students to draw on what they already know about a subject and encourages them to make connections. Because it focuses each student on what he or she wants to learn, the KWL chart engages each student in the learning process. Finally, after reading, it gives students a place to reflect on what they have learned.

Get Behind the Scenes: Finding Key Information—5W's and H

Students can use this organizer during reading as a note-taking tool or after reading to gather their thoughts and check their comprehension. This organizer gives students a space to collect key information about a subject. Because it requires additional thinking, it takes students beyond the traditional 5 W's and is an easy way to connect reading and writing. Students can use this graphic organizer to brainstorm their own ideas before writing.

Fact or Opinion?: Identifying Fact and Opinion

Differentiating between fact and opinion is an important skill for developing readers. They need to identify factual statements as those that can be supported by evidence and opinion statements as those that are expressions of a person's beliefs. Teaching students to make this distinction is critical and requires lots of practice.

Use this organizer to help students determine if interesting information is fact or opinion. You can direct students to find two facts, two opinions, or one of each. Or you can allow them to choose any statements they want and then classify them. You could also give students statements to illustrate and then determine if they're fact or opinion; this is a useful prereading or review strategy.

Venn Diagram: Compare and Contrast

A Venn diagram can help students compare and contrast two characters, settings, events, or other literary elements. This simple graphic organizer highlights similarities and differences, making it easy for students to think about how they organized the information. In groups, students can share and compare the information on their Venn diagrams. Younger students can draw pictures to represent ideas and discuss their drawings with a reading partner.

Build With Details: Main Idea and Details

This graphic organizer helps students sort out the big idea and the smaller details that support that big idea. It works best with nonfiction texts such as magazine articles, biographies, and textbooks. Students can use this organizer while they are reading to take notes and organize their ideas. Or, they can use it after reading to recall the important information. This organizer is a great tool to introduce students to paragraph writing. The main idea transforms into the topic sentence, and the details become supporting sentences.

Name: _____ Date: _____

My Personal Thinking and Learning Record

DIRECTIONS:

1. Before you read, write down everything you already know about the topic in the **What I Know** box.

2. Then write questions you have about the topic in the **What I Want to Know** box.

3. After you read, write important information and answers to your questions in the **What I Learned** box.

Topic: _____

K What I **K**now	**W** What I **W**ant to Know	**L** What I **L**earned

Name: _____ Date: _____

Get Behind the Scenes

DIRECTIONS:

1. Write the article's subject in the Subject Box.

2. After reading, draw and write notes that answer each question in the boxes. This step will help you identify the 5W's and H: Who, What, Where, When, Why, and How.

Take One Subject: _____

Who? _____

Where? _____
When? _____

What happened? Why? _____

How did it end? _____

Name: _____ Date: _____

Fact or Opinion?

DIRECTIONS:

1. Read the book or article all the way through. Highlight at least two interesting statements.

2. Choose two interesting statements and draw them in the boxes below.

3. Write a caption for each picture. Then decide if the statement is a fact or an opinion. Label each picture as fact or opinion.

1. Caption: _____

_____

_____

_____

Label: _____

2. Caption: _____

_____

_____

_____

Label: _____

Name: _____   Date: _____

Venn Diagram

DIRECTIONS:

1. Read the book or article all the way through.

2. Write the two people, places, or things to compare in the circles.

3. Draw or write shared traits in the center where the circles overlap.

4. Draw or write unique traits in each circle.

Title and author: _____

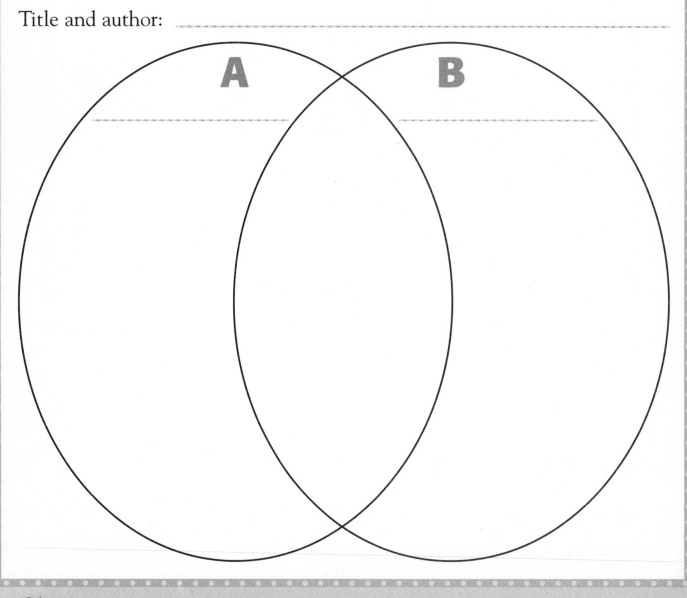

Name: _____   Date: _____

Build With Details

DIRECTIONS:

1. Preview the article or book to see what you can learn about the topic. Read the title and first and last sentences. Look at any pictures, charts, or words in bold.

2. Read the article or book all the way through. Write the title in the space below.

3. List the details the writer gives about the subject in the separate boxes.

4. Add all of the details up to find out what the main idea is. Write it below.

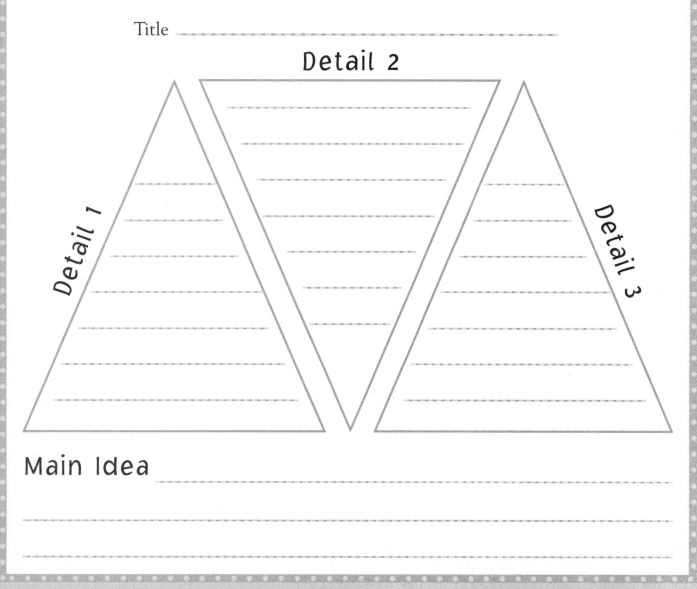

Title _____

Detail 2

Detail 1

Detail 3

Main Idea _____

_____

Strategies for Reading Poetry

Reading poetry is different from reading fiction and nonfiction. Poetry challenges readers to look at words closely, visualize, and listen to the sounds of words. Poetry is often a good place to start looking for meaning in writing. Because of the condensed form of the poem, many students will not feel afraid of jumping right in. The two organizers in this section will invite your students to be active readers as they respond to poetry.

Say It Your Way: Paraphrasing

Use this strategy with your students to examine particular lines of a poem. These can be lines that students liked or found surprising or difficult. Explain to students that when they paraphrase, they translate the author's words into their own. Impress upon students that the paraphrasing should be their own words and in their own style.

Hop on the Sensory Express: Noticing Sensory Details

Poetry is often packed with sensory images and details that call up vivid images in the reader's mind. To help your students get the most out of poetry, encourage them to pay close attention to words describing sights, sounds, smells, tastes, and touch. To capture the images these words trigger, have students sketch any pictures that pop into their heads. This strategy helps readers connect to the poems and focus on specific language. You can have students tape the two sheets together to create the Sensory Express.

Idea Box

Rereading

Encourage your students to read a poem many times.

1. The first reading should be for pure enjoyment.

2. During the second reading, students can look for clues to what the poem is saying.

3. Ask, "How does the poem make you feel?" on the third reading.

Idea Box

Paraphrasing

Students can paraphrase in a number of different situations. Encourage students to paraphrase during.

◎ class discussion.

◎ conversations with a reading partner.

◎ journal entries.

◎ summaries.

Name: _____ Date: _____

Say It Your Way

Talking about your ideas with others can help you understand a difficult phrase or line.

DIRECTIONS:

1. Read the poem out loud and to yourself several times.

2. As you read, put a sticky note beside a line you liked, found surprising, or one that you did not understand.

3. Write the line down in the megaphone.

4. Then write what you think the lines are saying in your own words.

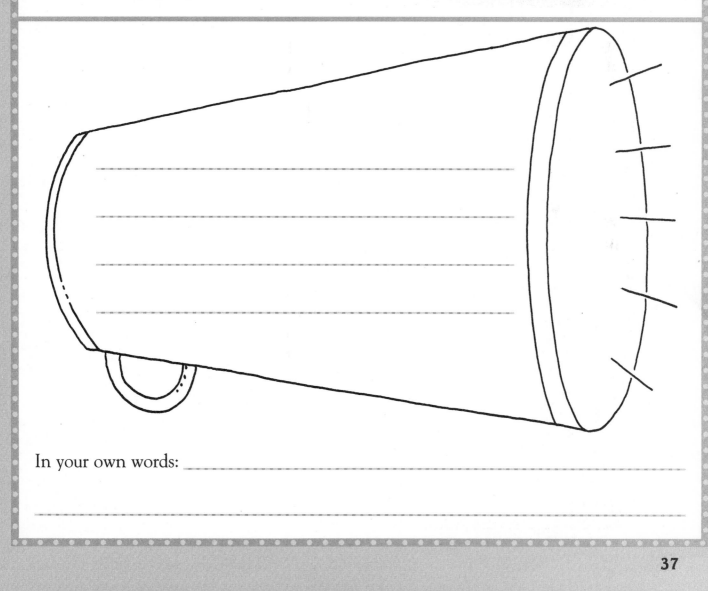

In your own words: _____
_____

Name: _____

Date: _____

Hop on the Sensory Express

DIRECTIONS:

1. Read the poem out loud and to yourself several times.

2. As you read, look out for words that appeal to your sight, hearing, smell, touch, and taste. Note: Every sense might not be in each poem.

3. Write the title and poet's name in the box below.

4. Write the words in the sense boxes.

5. Sketch the images that pop into your head when you read those words.

Sight Words

Poem: _____

Poet: _____

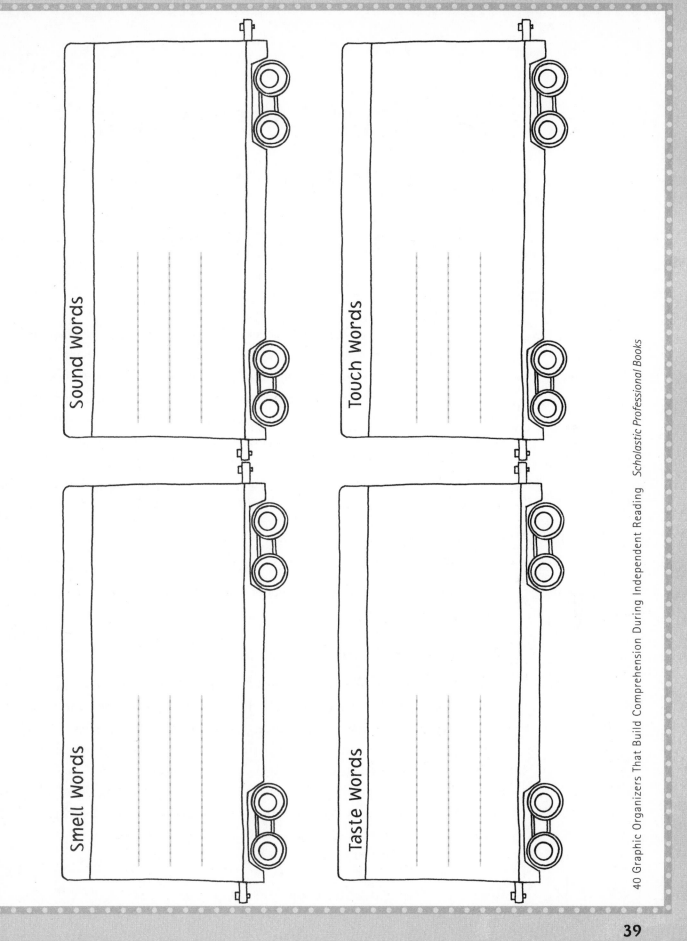

Sound Words

Touch Words

Smell Words

Taste Words

PART 4

Helping Students Understand Literary Genres

There are two main reasons for developing your students' grasp of different literary genres. First, understanding genre helps students know what to expect from a new text—how it is organized, what its purpose is—which boosts their comprehension. Second, understanding genre facilitates a reading and writing connection. When students know how a genre works, they can begin to write in that genre, incorporating its structure and elements. Help students see that a genre is a category or a kind of literature. Give them examples of different genres like fantasy, fairy tales, biography, and so on. The graphic organizers in this section deepen students' understanding of fiction, folk and fairy tales, nonfiction, and poetry.

Fiction

The graphic organizers grouped under fiction can be used interchangeably with realistic fiction, historical fiction, and fantasy.

Paint a Portrait: Character Map

Getting to know the different characters in stories and books is one of the best parts of reading. Help students dig into characters by paying attention to these details: a character's physical appearance, personality, speech, thoughts, feelings, actions, and interactions with other characters. Character maps help students keep track of facts and details and draw conclusions about a character. Students can use this graphic organizer during and after reading to record information about a character. You can also invite students to use the map as a brainstorming tool when they begin to write character sketches.

What a Character!: Double-Entry Journal

The double-entry journal is an effective way to assess how students are responding to the reading. With this double-entry journal, students visualize the main character and draw their image on one side. They then write about the character's personality on the other.

What's the Problem? Problem/Actions/Outcome

Stories are built around problems. Part of the excitement of reading comes from the desire to know how characters resolve the problems they face. Encourage students to focus on the actions that lead to the problem's resolution. This skill—finding connections between actions and outcomes—will help students make deeper connections between events in the text and focus students on the main events of a story. You can extend their thinking by asking them to write on the back of the sheet about other ways the problem could have been solved.

Follow the Footsteps: Sequence

To keep track of the events in a chapter or a story, it helps to use a sequence organizer. Tell students that when you can "see" the chain of events and keep track of the time order, you can remember what caused what in a story. Remind students that stories sometimes jump back and forth in time. Model for students with a Read Aloud how to sequence the main events of a story, pointing out the specific words that key you in to time order.

Map It Out: Story Structure

A story structure chart highlights the main parts of a story. It helps students sort out what is most important to focus on as they read. Use this organizer to help students identify the setting, main character, problem, and outcome.

Narrative Fan: Summarize

Encourage your students to be active thinkers as they read. Tell students that when they read, they are constantly getting new information. One way to keep track of this information is to record what they remember after they read. Use the Narrative Fan to get students to refer to the text, reread, and jog their memories.

This is a great tool to use to ensure that students make connections and monitor themselves as they read. You can also use the Narrative Fan to get students ready to write summaries.

Beginning to End: Character Development

One of the exciting things about reading is following how a character develops and what he or she learns. Point out to students that in most stories the main character learns something or changes from the way he or she acted or thought at the beginning. When students can grasp how a character grows and learns, they will be able to begin to understand theme.

Idea Box

Model the Narrative Fan

A. Read aloud a picture book.

B. As you read, point out when you get to a description of the setting, an important event, a problem, and the outcome.

C. After reading aloud, on large chart paper, create a "class fan." Display the fan so that students can refer to it for ideas.

Name: _____   Date: _____

Paint a Portrait

DIRECTIONS:

1. Read the story or book.

2. As you read, pay special attention to the main character.

3. After you read, draw and write about the character in the spaces below.

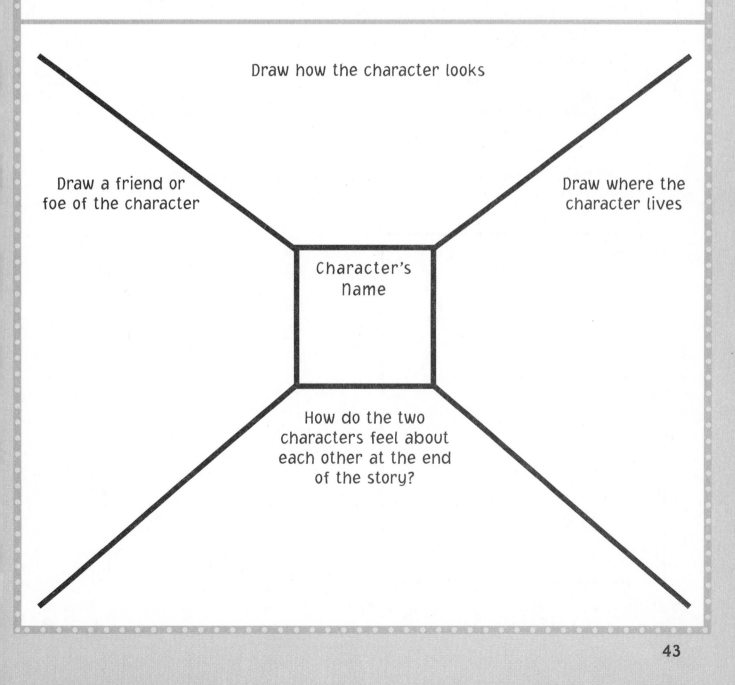

Draw how the character looks

Draw a friend or foe of the character

Draw where the character lives

Character's Name

How do the two characters feel about each other at the end of the story?

Name: _____ Date: _____

What a Character!

Idea Box

Clever, generous, dishonest, friendly, selfish, loyal, outgoing, mean, brave

DIRECTIONS:

1. As you read, think about the main character's personality. Choose one trait to describe him or her. (See the idea box for suggestions.)

2. After reading, draw the character in the box below using details from the story to help you.

3. Then, write about the character's personality below.

Visualize It

Sketch the character here.

Write About It

I think the character named

_____

is a _____

person. I think this because in the story he/she _____

_____

_____

_____

_____

_____

Name: _____   Date: _____

What's the Problem?

DIRECTIONS:

1. Read the story or book.

2. As you read, place a sticky note beside any big problems that occur.

3. After you read, sketch and write about one important problem the main character faced.

4. Then sketch and write about the outcome.

Problem	Outcome

The main problem was _____

_____

_____

_____

_____

The problem (was/was not) resolved by

_____

_____

_____

_____

Name: _____ Date: _____

Follow the Footsteps

DIRECTIONS:

1. Read a chapter.

2. As you read, think about the main events and the order in which they happened.

3. After you read, fill in footsteps with a a written explanation ,

Title _____

Author _____

Chapter title or number _____

Idea Box

Here are some key words that can signal time-order: **First, It started when, Second, Next, Then, Later, Now, As, After, Finally, Last, At the end**

Name: _____   Date: _____

Map It Out

DIRECTIONS:

1. As you read, keep track of the important details you learn by placing sticky notes next to clues about the setting, main character, an important problem, and the outcome.

2. After you read, draw the setting, main character, problem, and outcome below. Then write about each one.

Title _____   Author _____

Setting

This story takes place _____

Main Character

The main character is _____

Problem

The main problem is _____

Outcome

This is how it ends: _____

Name: _____ Date: _____

Narrative Fan

DIRECTIONS:

1. Read the story or book with a partner.
2. After you read, discuss the main events in the story with your partner.
3. Work together and record your ideas in the Narrative Fan.

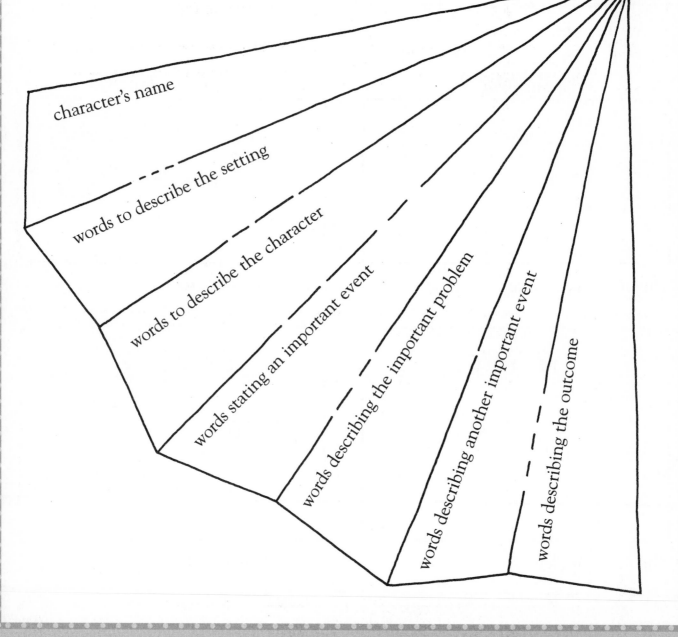

Name: _____ Date: _____

Beginning to End

DIRECTIONS:

1. Read the story or book.

2. Think about what the character was like at the beginning and end. Think about what made him or her grow or change.

3. After you read, draw and write about the character.

4. Then, explain what made the character grow or change.

Beginning	End

Write what the main character is like at the beginning: _____

_____

_____

Write what the main character is like at the end: _____

_____

_____

How did the character change? Why do you think he or she changed? _____

_____

_____

_____

Folk and Fairy Tales

Folktales and fairy tales are timeless stories that are read all over the world. This genre of literature grew out of the oral storytelling tradition, which started thousands of years ago. Many of these tales deal with issues and problems that all children face and can relate to no matter where they are from or when they live.

Are You Up to the Test?: Identifying Tasks

A "task" is a specific assignment or mission that a character must complete. Use this organizer to help your students define the tasks in a tale and understand how the tasks change the story. Tell your students that one of the defining characteristics of folk and fairy tales is that often a hero or heroine must complete a number of tasks or duties. These tasks often occur in threes and must be completed before the problem can be solved.

Magic Powers: Elements of Folk and Fairy Tales

Use this organizer to teach your students to recognize the forces of good and evil, in folk and fairy tales and to discover how these forces move the plot along. By understanding the elements of the genre, students will ultimately be able to synthesize the different parts of the story. In my classroom, I introduce the genre by reading aloud folk and fairy tales and discussing the magical elements and whether they are forces of good or evil.

Heros and Heroines With Heart: Inferring Character Traits

This organizer encourages students to think about a character by focusing on what the character says, does, or thinks and then inferring character traits. Ask students to describe the hero or heroine in their story, using the adjectives on the sheet to get their thinking started. For each character trait they choose, ask them to return to the story to find an action or speech that illustrates the trait.

You can use this organizer to make a reading and writing connection. When students write character sketches or character description paragraphs, they can include details about what the person says, does, or thinks to make their descriptions stronger.

Helping Students Understand Genre

Rumpelstiltskin
by Jonathan Langley, HarperCollins 1991

"Magic is an important part of this story. It is magical when the little man, Rumpelstiltskin, appears in the locked castle room from out of nowhere and can change straw into gold. His disappearance is magical, too. When the princess finds out his name and tells the little man it is Rumpelstiltskin, he gets angry and disappears. Even though Rumpelstiltskin helped the princess at first by changing the straw to gold, he ended up being an evil force because he wanted to take her baby away."

Name: _____ Date: _____

Are You Up to the Test?

DIRECTIONS:

1. As you read, look for the tasks the hero or heroine must complete.

2. After you read, describe two tasks in the boxes below. Write about the lesson the hero learned from each task.

Title _____ Name of Hero(ine) _____

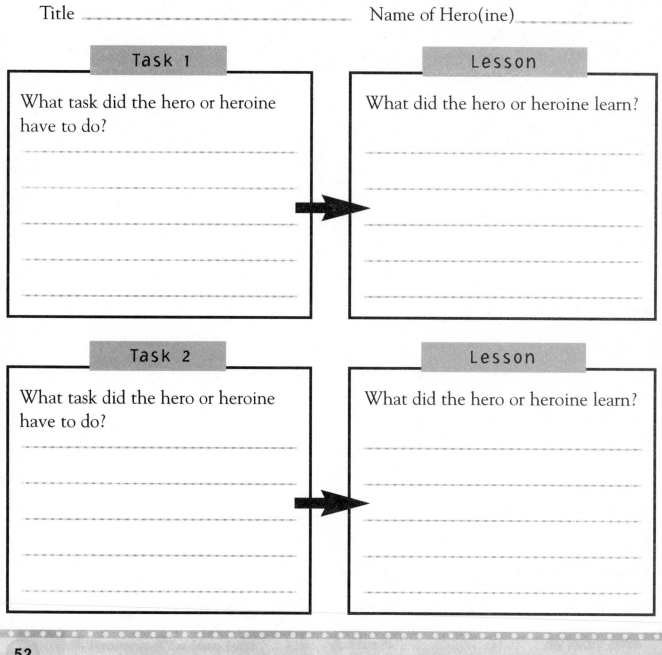

Task 1

What task did the hero or heroine have to do?

Lesson

What did the hero or heroine learn?

Task 2

What task did the hero or heroine have to do?

Lesson

What did the hero or heroine learn?

Name: _____   Date: _____

Magic Powers

DIRECTIONS:

1. Review the definition *forces of evil*.

2. As you read your story or book, look for the forces of good or evil.

3. Fill in the web below.

Definition
Forces of Evil: In many folk and fairy tales an evil force works against the hero or heroine to try to stop them from being happy. Example: the wicked queen in *Snow White*.

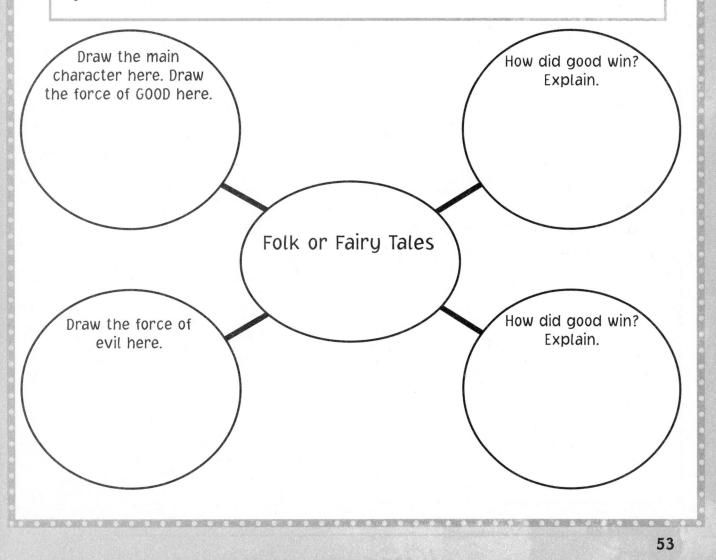

Draw the main character here. Draw the force of GOOD here.

How did good win? Explain.

Folk or Fairy Tales

Draw the force of evil here.

How did good win? Explain.

Name: _____ Date: _____

Heros and Heroines With Heart

DIRECTIONS:

1. As you read your story or book, look for what the hero or heroine says, does, or thinks that makes him or her a good hero.

2. Choose a word to describe the hero or heroine and write it below. Check out the idea box.

3. Draw a scene from the story that shows the hero or heroine acting the way you described him or her.

Idea Box

Here are some great words to describe a hero or heroine. These words are called character traits: **courageous, brave, strong, bold, spirited, daring, kind, firm, confident, adventurous**

Title _____ Author _____

Choose one word to describe the hero or heroine _____

Draw

Draw what the hero or heroine does, says, or thinks that proves he or she is this way.

I chose to describe the hero(ine) as

_____

because _____

_____

_____

_____

_____

_____

Poetry

Reading, enjoying, and understanding poetry is a delicious experience. Poets love words, and poems read aloud often light up children's faces. In my experience, avid as well as reluctant readers dive into poems eagerly. They love poetry's music, rhythm, images, and rhyme. Reading poems is an excellent way to motivate readers. Poems are usually shorter than prose and do not threaten students. They appeal to the senses and draw the reader into the poet's world immediately. In addition, poems are rhythmical and rock readers into an enjoyable place.

In school, students are often asked to decide what a poem "means." Encourage your students to focus first on the images or pictures that come into their mind after reading. Introduce them to the tools a poet uses to create those pictures. After students fall in love with the words, you can begin talking about meaning.

The graphic organizers in this section encourage students to reread, listen to sounds, and picture the images the poems paint. Each organizer focuses on an element of the craft of poetry.

What Is It Like?: Simile

A simile is a comparison between two unlike things using the words *like* or *as*. A simile is a figure of speech that helps readers see an idea in a new way. Use this graphic organizer to help students locate and define similes in poems. It is also a good tool to use in connection to writing workshop. Students can use the similes they create or decipher on this page as springboards for their own poetry. I often think aloud about creating similes to help my students understand this figure of speech better; see the model Think Aloud on this page.

Think Aloud

Using Similes

"When I hear the line *The wind was fast*, I don't get a very clear picture in my head. My idea of fast might be very different from your idea of fast. So I am going to try to think of some other thing that has something in common with the fast wind, for instance a jet airplane, time when I'm opening birthday presents, an eye blinking. After I come up with some things I can compare the fastness of the wind to, I can rewrite my sentence using a simile: *The wind, like a jet airplane, blew past me.* How does this simile improve the image of the wind? Can you think of other similes that might work?"

Show Off the Shape: Concrete Poetry

A concrete or shape poem takes the shape of the object or subject it describes. Concrete poetry is a great way to introduce students to the difference between the way prose looks on the page and the way a poem might look. Use this graphic organizer to teach that the shape of a poem can add to its meaning. Explain that poets always think about where a word on a line will go or if a word (or letter) might stand alone on a line. Use the second page in this set to guide students to write their own shape poem.

Trip Over Your Tongue: Alliteration

Alliteration is the repetition of the same consonant sound at the beginning of several words of a line of poetry. Your students will probably be most familiar with the use of alliteration in tongue twisters, which make a fun introduction to this literary element. Tongue twisters often create a silly or funny mood by using so many repeated sounds. Poets use alliteration to create music and mood, and the use of alliteration in poetry is often more spare and subtle than in tongue twisters.

Meaningful Sounds: Onomatopoeia

Onomatopoeia is the use of words that sound like the noises they describe. Poets often use onomatopoeia to add fun or emphasis to the words they use. Sounds can transport you to a certain place and reinforce the meaning of the words.

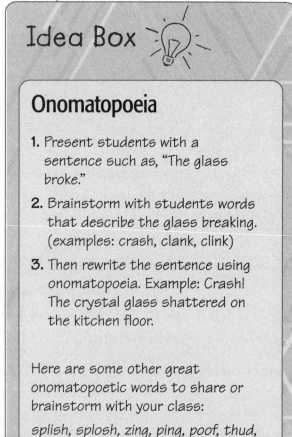

Idea Box

Onomatopoeia

1. Present students with a sentence such as, "The glass broke."

2. Brainstorm with students words that describe the glass breaking. (examples: crash, clank, clink)

3. Then rewrite the sentence using onomatopoeia. Example: Crash! The crystal glass shattered on the kitchen floor.

Here are some other great onomatopoetic words to share or brainstorm with your class:

splish, splosh, zing, ping, poof, thud, crash, bam, splat, pop, pow, whack, eek, click, tick-tock, smack, wham, blam, rattle, zip, screech, plunk.

Name: _____ Date: _____

What Is It Like?

DIRECTIONS:

1. Read the poem out loud and to yourself several times.

2. As you read, look for similes; write one below. Answer the questions about your simile.

3. Explain the similes in the chart below.

4. After, reread the poem again and think about how the similes add to pictures you get in your mind; draw what you see in your imagination on the back of this page.

> ### Definition
>
> **Simile:** A simile is a comparison between two unlike things using the words *like* or *as.* Think about this line: "sand sifting through my fingers like light snow." How is sand like snow? They are both fine and pale. You can pile both of them up. They both tickle your nose.

Title: _____

Author: _____

1. **Write the simile here.** _____

_____

_____

2. **What two things are being compared?** _____

_____

_____

3. **How are they alike?** _____

_____

_____

_____

Name: _____ Date: _____

Show Off the Shape

DIRECTIONS:

1. Read the poem "Above the Clouds" out loud and to yourself several times.

2. As you read, ask yourself how the poem's shape adds to its meaning.

3. Answer the questions below.

Definition

A concrete poem is a special form of poetry. Concrete poems are shape poems. They have the shape of the object the poem is about—a poem about football would be in the shape of a football; a poem about a sailboat might be in the shape of a sail.

Above the Clouds

so close to the clouds,

blue mountain   I feel like

up the   I could almost

Hiking   touch the sky.

1. What shape do the words of the poem make? _____

_____

2. How does the shape help you understand or enjoy the poem? _____

_____

Name: _____   Date: _____

Show Off the Shape 2

DIRECTIONS:

1. Choose a topic from the list at right or make up your own.

2. Draw the shape of the object in the sketch box.

3. Brainstorm words that describe your object, what your object does, or what is done with it. Write them in the brainstorm box.

4. Write your Concrete Poem on blank paper, using your sketch and brainstormed words to get you started.

Topics

sun, tree, baseball bat, airplane, cloud, star, rainbow, butterfly, bubbles, lollipop, alligator, book, kite, umbrella, arrow

Sketch

Sketch your object here

Brainstorm

Brainstorm words here

Name: _____ Date: _____

Trip Over Your Tongue

DIRECTIONS:

1. Read the Model Poem and review the definition of alliteration.

2. Then read your poem out loud and to yourself several times.

3. As you read, listen for any repeated consonant sounds at the beginning of words.

4. Answer the questions below about your poem.

(Model Poem)

Making Cookies

Nothing is sweeter than a Saturday
Covered in sugar and semi-sweet chocolate chips
And the chance that soon
I'll get to lick the sweet, sweet spoon.

Title _____ Author _____

1. What words start with the same sound? _____

_____

2. What "sound effect" does repeating that letter make? _____

_____

Name: _____ Date: _____

Meaningful Sounds

DIRECTIONS:

1. Read the Model Poem and review the definition of onomatopoeia.

2. Then read your poem out loud and to yourself several times.

3. As you read, listen for any onomatopoeia sounds.

4. Complete the second page of this sheet.

Model Poem

Swinging

Tick-tock,
I'm a grandfather clock
counting the seconds
swinging.

Swish, swish,
I'm a brave explorer
floating on vines
through the forest.

Whisk, whisk
I'm a trapeze artist
soaring above crowds
of squirrels.

Whee, whee
I'm a little girl
gliding over gardens
to the sky.

Definition

Onomatopoeia: Onomatopoeia is the use of words that sound like the noises they describe. In the poem "Swinging" each stanza begins with onomatopoeia. *Tick-tock* sounds like a clock; the word *swish* sounds like a vine swinging; the word *whisk* sounds like the noise a trapeze flying through the air might make; the word *whee* is the sound a child might make when the swing goes high.

Meaningful Sounds

Title _____   Poet _____

1. **What words are onomatopoetic?**

_____

_____

_____

_____

2. **How do they help
you imagine the scene?**

_____

_____

_____

_____

3. **Draw what you see in
your mind here.**

Idea Box

breaking glass,
chewing ice, wet socks,
sneezing, wind blowing,
belly flopping in a pool,
airplane taking off,
traffic jam

Try It Out!

Write your own onomatopoetic lines.

1. Choose a topic from the box or use your own.

2. Brainstorm a list of words that describe the sound.

3. Write the sounds into sentences.

_____

_____

_____

_____

Nonfiction

Begin your study of nonfiction by guiding your class through a KWL. This activity will help you assess what they already know and plan what nonfiction genres to work with. Make sure students know that nonfiction as a category or genre of literature encompasses biography, memoir, articles in newspapers and magazines, science books, informational picture and chapter books, and so on. Curiosity and the desire to learn about the world around them attract students to non-fiction. Use the graphic organizers in this section to focus them on the important elements of this genre.

Students will encounter nonfiction reading material in all subjects and on standardized tests. When students understand the structure of expository texts, they can more readily navigate through them and recall facts from magazines, newspapers, and informational picture and chapter books.

Review how to preview a book (see page 18). Invite students to read and think about the title, pictures, captions, headings, maps, and graphs. Then, ask students to predict what they will learn.

Model It

Taking Notes

Explain to students how to take notes on sticky notes. Model for them as you read aloud how you would take notes. I often say something like:

"Sometimes I like to place sticky notes on a page in a book where I learned new information or discovered a new word. Marking the story with sticky notes makes it easier for me to go back and review the new information I learned. I use sticky notes in my journal sometimes, too. I take notes and write the page number of the book on my sticky notes so I can easily find and reread the passage."

The Road to Success: Biography

Use this organizer to help your students identify the key accomplishments in a person's life. The organizer asks students to describe one important accomplishment and decide if they admire the person or not, thereby helping them make personal connections to the text.

Fact-O-Gram: Informational Books

Informational books present students with a lot of new information. Students who can point out new information and organize it in their heads and in writing will be more successful at retaining the new information. Use this organizer either during reading for students to take notes on or after reading as an assessment of recall and comprehension.

I Wonder . . .: Questioning

Students who are active readers remain engaged in the text by constantly asking questions about what they are understanding and not understanding. This organizer will help students keep new ideas in their heads and sort out challenging information. Questioning is a great strategy to use before, during, and after reading. It helps students pinpoint what they understand and parts that confuse them. You can have students tape the two sheets together to create the sequence string.

Keep-in-Time . . .: Chronological Order

Chronological order is the arrangement of events in time order. Nonfiction texts often explain events or processes in the order in which they actually occurred. Use this graphic organizer to measure how well students can sequence events. You can have students tape the two sheets together to create the sequence string.

Once I . . .: Making Connections

To deepen students' understanding and enjoyment of reading informational texts, encourage them to make personal connections to the topics and new information they learn.

Treasure Hunt: Elements of Newspapers and Magazines

Use this organizer to help your students identify the different kinds of information they can find in a newspaper or magazine. Students who are aware of the organization of newspapers and magazines can evaluate the information, make choices about what to read, and form their own opinions.

Read All About It!: The 5W's and the News

Use this graphic organizer to help students identify the main points of a newspaper article. Model for students how you would preview an article before reading with the sample on page 72. Point out the headline, author, photos, repeated words, and graphs and charts. Tell students that a quick preview of an article can often help them learn a lot of important information. Keep reading articles about many different subjects until students can find the facts with ease. Then, make the reading and writing connection by using this organizer as a plan for students to write their own newspaper articles.

Name: _____ Date: _____

The Road to Success

DIRECTIONS:

1. Read the biography or autobiography.

2. As you read, look for the important events in this person's life.

3. After you read, write and draw about one important event in the person's life.

Person's Name

Draw one important
accomplishment
in this person's life.

Explain your drawing.

_____

_____

_____

_____

Keep Thinking

Do you admire this person? Why? Why not? Write about it on the back.

Name: _____ Date: _____

Fact-O-Gram

DIRECTIONS:

1. Read the book or article

2. As you read, keep track of new facts you learn by putting sticky notes beside them.

3. After you read, think about how you would explain these facts to someone. Record one of your ideas in the telegraph below.

HOWDY _____ !

In a book called _____ ,

I found out that _____

_____

_____

_____

_____

Keep Thinking

What else would you like to learn about this subject? _____

_____

Where could you look to find it out? _____

_____

PAIR-AND-SHARE: Discuss what you learned with a reading partner.

Name: _____ Date: _____

I Wonder . . .

DIRECTIONS:

1. Before you read, answer the first question below. Then read the book or article.

2. As you read, think about the questions that pop into your head.

3. After, record your questions and thoughts below.

What do I already know about this subject? _____

_____

After Reading: What questions do you still have?
How
What
Are there
Why

Name: _____ Date: _____

Keep-in-Time Sequence String

DIRECTIONS:

1. Read the chapter or article.
2. As you read, pay attention to the order in which things happen.
3. Write and draw about four important events in order on the sequence string below.

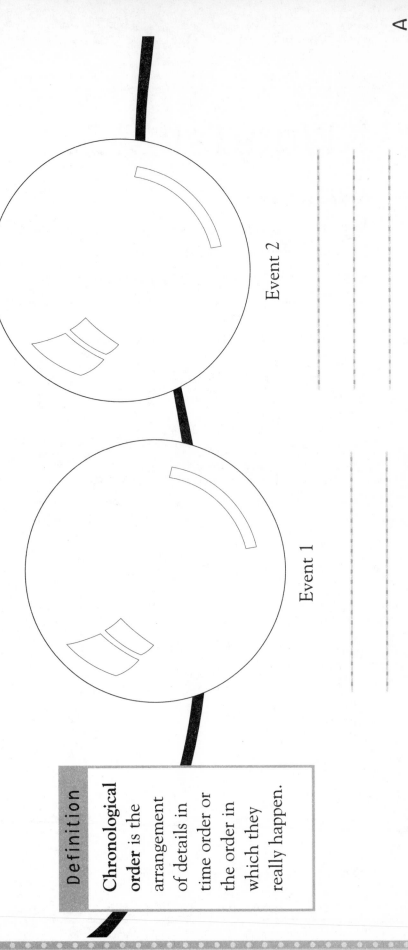

Event 1

Event 2

Definition

Chronological order is the arrangement of details in time order or the order in which they really happen.

A

68

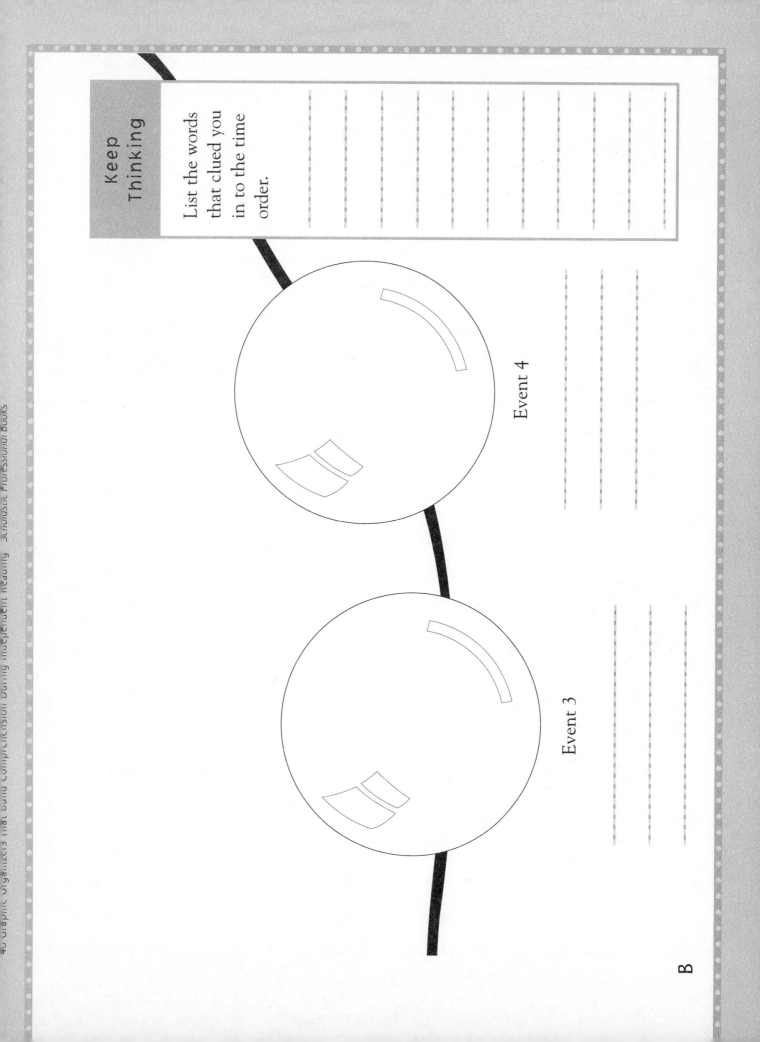

Keep
Thinking

List the words
that clued you
in to the time
order.

Event 4

Event 3

Name: _____ Date: _____

Once I . . .

DIRECTIONS:

1. Read the text.

2. As you read, use sticky notes to mark information that you connect to.

3. Record your connections in the chart below.

Kind of Information	Draw It	Connections I Made
The new information I connected to was		I made this connection because
The photo or illustration I connected to was of		I made this connection because
The map/chart/graph that I connected to was of		I made this connection because

70

Name: _____   Date: _____

Treasure Hunt

DIRECTIONS:

1. Skim through a newspaper or a magazine.

2. As you skim, look for the different kinds of information you can find.

3. Then fill the treasure chest with all the things you can learn from the newspaper or magazine.

Idea Box

Newspapers can fill you in on what is happening in the world or what is happening at your library tonight. Look for headlines, bold words, photos and captions, maps, diagrams, and charts.

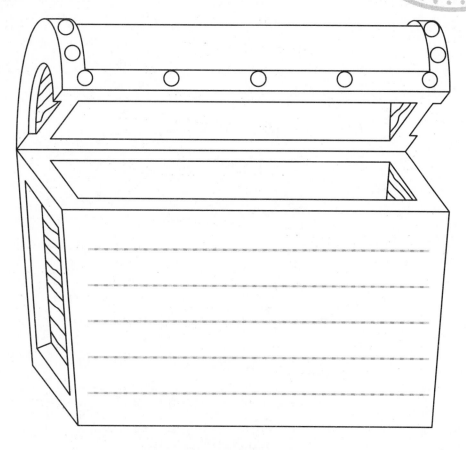

Keep Thinking

What did you find that surprised you?

_____

Name: _____   Date: _____

Read All About It!

DIRECTIONS:

1. Preview a newspaper article.

2. Now read the article and see how many of the 5W's you can answer.

3. After, draw and write to fill in the organizer with the information you learned.

Preview Tip

Make sure you check out the headline and author, photos, captions, maps, graphs, and charts.

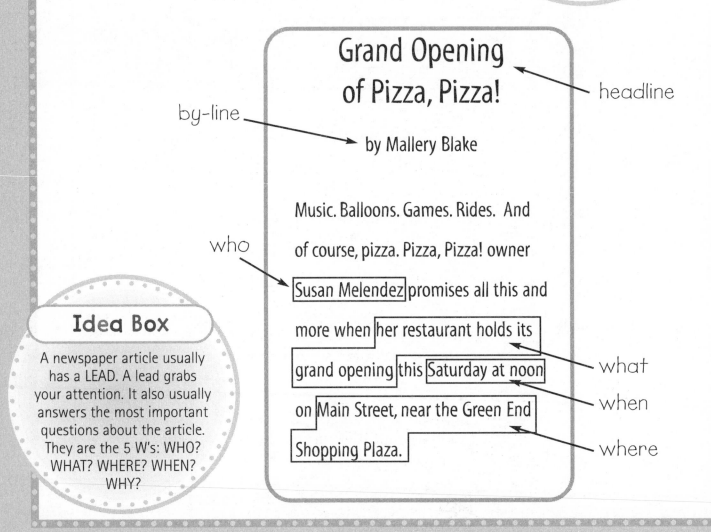

Grand Opening of Pizza, Pizza! ← headline

by-line → by Mallery Blake

Music. Balloons. Games. Rides. And of course, pizza. Pizza, Pizza! owner

who → Susan Melendez promises all this and

more when her restaurant holds its

grand opening this Saturday at noon — what — when

on Main Street, near the Green End

Shopping Plaza. — where

Idea Box

A newspaper article usually has a LEAD. A lead grabs your attention. It also usually answers the most important questions about the article. They are the 5 W's: WHO? WHAT? WHERE? WHEN? WHY?

Read All About It!

Article: _____

- Who
- What
- Where
- When
- Why

PART 5

Reading and Word Study

Vocabulary and word study activities can be continued throughout an independent reading program. As students read and challenge themselves with different genres and harder texts, they encounter words that they do not know. Armed with strategies, students can approach new vocabulary with confidence. Students can study words in every genre that they read.

Show students how thinking about context clues and clues from illustrations or charts helps them become word sleuths. Instead of feeling only frustration when faced with new vocabulary, students can feel success. Here are some guidelines to help your students become word detectives:

- Have students write two to three new words that they found tough on a sticky note.

- Ask students to write the page number on which they found each word.

- Show students how you use context clues to figure out a word's meaning.

- Repeat your modeling and think aloud many times.

Invite students to help you use context clues. Once students "get it," have them work in pairs to figure out their words' meanings.

What I Know About Words: Using Prior Knowledge

Often students know more about new words than they realize. Encourage them to stop and take some time with an unfamiliar word. Model how you would think about a new word, pointing out its different parts as well as picture and context clues in the story. Tell students that often you can get the gist of a word without having to look it up in a dictionary.

Web a Word: Word Questioning

Encourage your students to actively question themselves about words as they read. This wondering keeps students involved in the story and ensures that they are not simply sounding out words but comprehending them. Model asking questions about words as you read a storybook aloud.

Word Questioning: *glistening*

Think Aloud

Rumpelstiltskin
by Jonathan Langley, HarperCollins 1991

"In the story I read, 'all the straw was gone and in its place was a heap of glistening gold.' Glistening isn't a word that I have heard before. I wonder what it means. If I look at the picture, I see the big pile of gold and there are gold, sunny rays coming off of it just like it was a sun. Gold is like the sun because they are both yellow and they both shine. Maybe glistening means something like shining or sparkling."

Word Links: Making Connections

Words studied and memorized from lists rarely make it into a student's vocabulary. However, when students can connect a word to their life, they make the word their own. With this organizer, students explore a new word from their reading. Have them brainstorm examples of people, places, things, events, and situations where this word might be used, encouraging them to make personal connections to the word.

Words in the World: Sensory Language Chart

This organizer is a great way to help students focus on how sensory language can enrich a story or poem. Invite students to gather details from stories or poems that relate to the five senses: sight, smell, taste, touch, and sound. Sensory language helps students visualize words in their heads, giving them a deeper understanding of their meaning and providing a great way to remember the word. Developing a concrete association with a word helps them retain it longer. Brainstorm word lists with your students that appeal to different senses. You can connect this strategy to a writing lesson by using the strong, concrete sense words to write list poems that appeal to the different senses.

Name: _____ Date: _____

What I Know About Words

DIRECTIONS:

1. When you come to a word that you don't know, write it in the chart.

2. Think about what you know about the word. Does it have a prefix or suffix you know? Is there a root word? Can you tell if it's a noun, verb, or adjective? Write what you know about the word.

3. Look at the pictures for clues. Write these clues below.

4. From what you know, the picture clues, and your reading, write what you think the word might mean.

Word 1	Word 2
_____	_____
What I know about this word: _____	What I know about this word: _____
_____	_____
_____	_____
Picture clues tell me:	Picture clues tell me:
_____	_____
_____	_____
_____	_____
This word might mean	This word might mean
_____	_____
_____	_____

Name: _____ Date: _____

Web a Word

DIRECTIONS:

1. When you come to a word that you don't know, write it in the chart.

2. Answer the questions in the web to help you think about the word.

3. Keep reading to find clues about the meaning; add new information to the web.

4. Write what you think the word means.

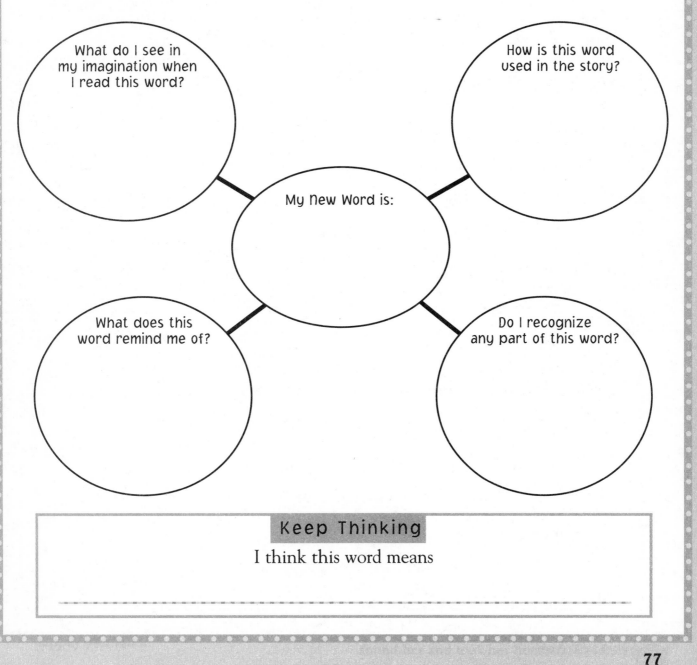

What do I see in my imagination when I read this word?

How is this word used in the story?

My New Word is:

What does this word remind me of?

Do I recognize any part of this word?

Keep Thinking

I think this word means

77

Name: _____ Date: _____

Word Links

DIRECTIONS:

1. Write the new word below.

2. Complete the sheet to help you make connections to the new word.

Word _____

Sentence the word is used in: _____

_____

_____

Other places I might find this word: _____

_____

I might use this word: _____

_____

_____

I'm going to remember this word by connecting it to: _____

_____

_____

_____

What it means: _____

_____

Name: _____ Date: _____

Words in the World

DIRECTIONS:

1. Read the story.

2. When you come to a word that makes you use one of your senses, write it in the chart under that sense.

3. Write what the words make you see in your mind in the middle of the column.

4. Write other words that remind you of the new word in the third column.

Title: _____ Author: _____

Sense Words	What I Imagine	Other Words That I Know That Are Similar
Sight		
Sound		
Smell		
Taste		
Touch		

Professional Resources

Fielding and Pearson: *Education Leadership*, 51 (5), 1994.

Richard Allington: *The Elementary School Journal*, Vol. 83, 1983.

Nagy, William E., 1988. *Teaching Vocabulary to Improve Reading Comprehension*, NCTE & IRA.

Vacca, R.T. & J.L. Vacca, 1999. *Content Area Reading: Literacy and Learning Across the Curriculum*, 16th Ed. NY: Longman.